LIQUIDATIONS MANUAL

(Buying and Selling Consumer Products for up to 85% off)

By Clifford Woods

COPYRIGHT

© 1998, 1999, 2000, 2001, 2013, 2015 and 2016 by Clifford Woods

All rights reserved. No part of this publication may be reproduced, distributed, or transmitted in any form or by any means, including photocopying, recording, or other electronic or mechanical methods, without the prior written permission of the publisher, except in the case of brief quotations embodied in critical reviews and certain other non-commercial uses permitted by copyright law.

CREATE SPACE

Table of Contents

Introduction [3]

Chapter 1: Basic Definitions [6]

Chapter 2: What are consumer products? [8]

Chapter 3: How to find products [12]

Mailing Lists [19]

Chapter 4: Submitting Products [21]

Summary [22]

Bonus [24]

Sample Postcard Text [25]

Sample Letter/Fax/Email [26]

Questions and Answers [27]

Special Addition: Finding Buyers and Sellers [32]

Becoming a Broker [36]

Thank You [37]

About the Author [38]

The Liquidation Business

Introduction

The Liquidation business is a very simple, fun and interesting business to do.

Let's start with the liquidation story:

The Liquidation Story – Why will this business will ALWAYS be viable – not matter the state of the economy:

Want to knock off someone?

Consumer Liquidations! No, it's not assassinations for sale! We are talking about the business of locating overstocked, unwanted or discontinued consumer products at a fraction of what it cost the manufacturing company to make it.

Oh. How is this possible? I'll tell you. Let's start with how come the liquidation business exists in the first place. There is well over 60,000 Completed Consumer Manufacturing Companies in the Continental United States.

By this I mean that these companies make things like watches, leather goods, purses, gold and silver jewelry, books, household appliances, sporting goods, canned foods televisions, radios etc. and they are all packaged and ready to be put on a shelf in a retail store for sale.

Now, at times and due to various reasons, too much of an item is made by mistake. I am talking about one hundred thousand or a half a million items too much. For example, products are made and the customer ordering them goes bankrupt before taking delivery and so on.

Manufacturing companies are then left with unwanted, discontinued or overstocked items. Usually these items are unique to the customer they make them for. These unwanted products take up warehouse space, which the manufacturer vitally needs to store other products for active customers. For this reason, the manufacturing companies have a very high motivation to get rid of these products.

Usually the manufacturing company will write the expenses of producing these products off as a tax loss, so anything he/she can get for them is a bonus of sorts. In the Liquidation business, the manufacturing companies normally sell these products to liquidation companies and individuals for about 10 percent or less of the retail value or 30% of the manufacturing cost.

Like any business, there are pitfalls to watch out for! You can buy a manual for about $300.00. Then spend another $100.00 on phone consultation and just about the time you are about to spend more money, find out that the products that you have been finding and sending off to the company you bought the manual from, ARE NOT BEING SOLD. By the time you wise up, you could be out $500.00 plus.

When you get through the pitfalls or find someone who has been through them, there are bonuses! Yes – there is a bonus. The liquidation business is exciting, interesting and very rewarding. In doing the locating of products, you will be receiving a half a dozen sample of each inventory you work with.

Three of these will be sent on to the company you work with. These samples are not returned. However you still have 3 samples on hand. What you do with them is entirely up to you. You could send them out to other buyers you yourself have personally collected to see if they are interested, give them away as presents or sell them. If you sell them, be sure to get your seller's license! Most of all have fun with it! Clifford Woods.

In the liquidation business, the manufacturing companies normally sell these products to Liquidators for 10% of the retail value, 15% of wholesale value or 30% of the manufacturing cost - NO MORE THAN THAT!

This manual will cover:

•Basic definitions used in the business.

•Consumer products - what they are and what they are not.

•How to find consumer products.

•Submitting products located to Rapid-Liquidations, a liquidation products buying and selling company.

It's an exciting, interesting and fun business - enjoy it!

CHAPTER 1

Basic definitions used in the business:

•Locator: A person who finds (locates) products that a Manufacturer wants to sell. These products by definition are unwanted, discontinued or overstocked and needs to be sold.

•Manufacturer: A person or company who actually makes the products.

•Liquidator: A company or person who buys unwanted, overstocked or discontinued merchandise from a Manufacturer or Distributor at liquidation prices and then sells these products on to others.

•Broker: A person who acts on behalf of the owner of an inventory and finds a buyer. The Inventory owner normally pays him a percentage of what he sells the products for.

•Retail price: This is what the product is sold for in a retail outlet that sells directly to the public (consumer).

•Wholesale price: This is the price that the manufacturer or distributor sells the products to the retail outlet for.

•Manufactured Cost: This is what it cost the manufacturer to make the product or what it cost the owner to have the products made and imported into this country.

•Liquidation price: Products bought at or below 10% of retail price or 15% of wholesale cost or 30% of the manufactured price. Normally it would be the lowest of the above prices.

- Consumer products: These are completed, retail ready products that can simply be placed on a shelf in a store and sold without anything else being done to them other than adding a price sticker.

- Bulk Products: These are products that are NOT retail ready and would have to be made retail ready before they could be sold in a retail outlet.

- F.O.B. This means "free on board" and a location is mentioned after it, for example, "FOB Miami". This means that the seller will put the inventory on board a transport in Miami (free of charge) and the buyer needs to pay to have it shipped to wherever the buyer wants the products. FOB Plant usually means that the buyer pays all shipping charges.

- FOB Destination means that the seller pays all shipping charges.

- Close Out: This term refers to products being sold at a discount by a store or distributor so as to get rid of stock on hand fast and recover some profit. It is NOT the same as liquidation prices. Liquidation prices are defined above.

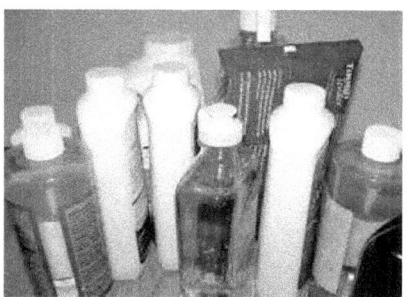

CHAPTER 2

What are Consumer Products?

So, what are consumer products as far as the liquidation business is concerned?

In this case, consumer products would be completed products that are retail ready and can simply be placed in a retail outlet, on the shelf, and sold. The only thing the retailer would need to add would be the retail price sticker.

As these products are mainly going to be sold to chains of discount stores, it is best that the inventory be all of the same type. For example if the inventory is watches, you would be interested if you had, say, 5000 of the SAME TYPE OF WATCH.

The reason for this is that when a sample is sent to the buyer - he KNOWS exactly what we are asking him to buy and this will make selling the inventory easier. If you had, 50 or 100 different TYPES of watches making up that 5000 inventory it would be much more difficult to sell. Therefore, you are primarily looking for inventories of the same type of consumer products.

Some examples of completed consumer products would be as follows:

- Watches
- leather goods
- purses, gold and silver jewelry
- ladies purses
- books

- household appliances
- small office equipment
- camera's
- gift ware
- outdoor and garden furniture
- hand tools
- sporting goods
- canned foods
- televisions
- radios
- clocks
- batteries

- toys
- garden equipment
- stationary
- bicycles
- computers
- camping equipment
- baseball caps (*Baseball caps have a special price of $3.00 or less for a dozen) and other things like these.

In short, anything that is retail ready can be sold in a retail outlet.

Exception

There are some exceptions as follows:

•perfumes

•posters

•cards

•cosmetics

•belts and scarves

The retail prices for these are so far above what they cost to manufacture, that even if you were to purchase them at the liquidation prices, they would be very hard to sell.

Therefore - do not bother with these.

Specials

Some items should only be purchased at special prices as listed here.

Reason:

The market is usually flooded with these and therefore the purchase price has to be very very low to sell them.

These special items are:

•cassette tapes: $.04 cents each

•sunglasses: $.15 cents each

•books: 4% or less of its retail price

- videotapes: $.60 cents each

- music CDs: $.45 cents each

- socks: $1.00 per dozen,

- t-shirts: $5.00 per dozen

- coffee mugs: $.10 each.

This is the basic on consumer products. Stay away from bulk products, as they are difficult to sell in the consumer market.

CHAPTER 3

HOW to Locate (find) Consumer Products:

OK. Now, how does one go about finding these fabulous consumer products at liquidation prices?

As mentioned, Manufacturing and Distribution companies have these in their warehouses and very much want to get rid of them. The reason the manufacturers are interested in getting rid of the product is that they are taking up vitally needed warehouse space and they have already written them off as tax loss.

Additionally, these products, sitting in their warehouses - reminds them of a failure.

There are two basic ways to find these products: by telephone and by mail/email. The best way I have found to locate products is by doing a combination of both telephone and mail/email. The reason for this is that with the telephone you find inventories right away, with the mail/email, the companies file your letter or post card to them, and you get inventories later as they become available.

Locating by telephone:

To locate consumer products by telephone, at no cost to you, all you need is a telephone and an 800 yellow page directory from AT&T. The directory (AT&T National Toll - Free Directory) can be ordered over the telephone from AT&T. It is not expensive. These days there are various Internet 800 number listings for the USA as well.

Other directories are available that you can use. I have found this one works just fine. The good thing about it is that if you take your time and call every company in the 800 yellow pages, by the time you get to the end, it's time to start calling from the beginning again!

This business never seems to "run dry". The reason for this is that these companies are manufacturing products every day, errors do occur, companies do go out of business, and product lines are discontinued. Therefore, you may call a company today and they do not have any unwanted inventory, but next week they do!

OK. Now you have your 800 yellow pages directory and your telephone and you are ready to start.

Here is what you do:

1. Open the yellow pages Directory to the first number listed under "Manufacturers" or "Wholesalers" or "Distributors" and dial the first number. Usually a receptionist answers.

2. You introduce yourself as _____ (your name) from XZY Liquidations (name of the company you have decided on). This can be your first name "Bob's Liquidations" or your last name "Brown's Liquidations" or any other name you choose.

3. The introduction would go something like this. "Hi, my name is Sara Mills and I'm calling from Direct Liquidations. May I please speak with the Lady or Gentleman that deals with liquidating excess merchandise?"

4. You will either be told to hold on; you will be put through to someone, and you will usually be told a name as well OR you will be told that the company does not liquidate its excess merchandise.

If this is the case, politely thank the receptionist, hang up, and call the next number in the book or on your list.

5. You may also be told that the person is out of the office. You have a choice here of leaving a voice mail for them or sending them your details by fax.

Leave a message and, if that is not possible, fax in one-page info on what your company does; see sample fax/letter at the end of this manual.

6. You are put through to the person who deals with liquidating excess merchandise. You introduce yourself again. "Hi, I'm Sara and I'm calling from Direct Liquidations. Are you the person that deals with liquidating excess merchandise?" Usually you get a "Yes, I am".

7. Your reply to this is something like "Great! I am calling you because we buy complete inventories of unwanted or discontinued merchandise for cash. Do you have any inventories around that you would like to liquidate?" Make sure you emphasize 'total inventories' and 'cash' as this gets their interest and makes them more willing to talk to you.

8. Usually you get something like "What sort of inventories are you looking for?"

9. Your reply is "Completed Consumer Merchandise".

10. The next thing you will hear is either "Yes - we have an inventory of _____ (something), would you be interested in that?" or "No we do not have anything like that".

11. If you get a 'no we do not have any consumer products', politely thanks the lady or gentleman, hang up and go on with the next call.

12. If you get a 'yes', your reply is "Let me ask you a few questions about it and get the following information:

- What is it? _____
- Where is it located _____
- How old is it? _____
- How are they packaged?
- Company name? _____
- What is the retail price? _____
- Wholesale price? _____
- Manufactured cost? _____

13. You will get the answers above easily - except possibly for manufactured cost, simply because some companies do not like to divulge what it cost them to produce something. Nevertheless, that is fine - just write down the information provided.

14. Then ask the lady or gentleman to hold a second and quickly calculate 10% of the retail price provided and 15% of the wholesale price and 30% of manufactured cost (if you get it) and note, which is lower.

15. Then say to the lady of gentleman, "Based on the information you have given me, we can make you a tentative offer of _____ (lower of the three prices calculated) for each item in this inventory". It's very important that you say "tentative" as you do not want to make firm offers until you KNOW you can sell this inventory!

16. The response is usually "That sounds good - what's next?"

17. To which you reply, "Send me half a dozen samples. I will get the information and samples out to my buyers and let you know the result as soon as possible."

18. Then you work out final details like the address to send the samples to and hang up the telephone. Note down the information in a log of some sort and continue calling.

19. When the samples arrive, submit them to Rapid Liquidations to sell or sell them yourself. (How to submit is covered later in this manual).

That is the basic cycle of locating consumer products by telephone at liquidation prices.

There are some other points worth mentioning as follows:

•If you are offered "closeout" items at anything above 10% of retail price or above 15% of wholesale price - DO NOT GET INVOLVED. The reason for this is that you will not be able to sell it easily.

•Make very sure that the products are retail ready and NOT BULK. Same reason as above - you will not be able to sell it easily in the consumer products liquidation business which is what we are involved in.

•NEVER pay for samples. If you are told that the samples will be sent out but you will be billed, your simple reply is "Sorry, our company policy is that we do not pay for samples of stocks we liquidate".

If this means that the deal falls through, that's okay. Just carry on and make your next call.

Otherwise, you will find yourself spending money you do not need to spend.

•When making calls, be sure to cross out telephone numbers where you have been told that the company does not liquidate products. This is so that you will not call those companies when you go through the 800 yellow pages again.

Locating Products by Mail/Email:

The other way to locate consumer products is by using the mail/email.

The best way I have found to do this is to get some post cards made up at a printer with your message on it. Purchase a mailing/email list of manufacturing companies from a mailing list house and send out cards/emails to manufacturing companies.

There are some basic rules when doing this to ensure that you get a response and that it is as cheap as possible to do.

These rules are:

1. Make very sure that the post card is of the right size for the Post Office to send out for the cheapest possible price. The Printer you use should know the size or you could check with the Post Office. The size I sent out that went through the post office at their best price was 3 1/2 inch high by 5 1/2 inch wide.

2. The card should be of a BRIGHT COLOR. This is so that it shows up easily in the other mail being received by the Manufacturers.

3. It should be printed on one side only - leave the other side blank for the mailing label and the postage stamp.

4. The top of the printed side should have the name of your company and a phrase next to it like this: "We buy your unwanted consumer items for CASH!"

5. Below that should be a line that says, "Please copy and pass to the Warehouse Manager, the Operations Manager, Inventory/Stock Manager and the Owner". This makes sure that the information gets to all possible people that would be interested in selling excess merchandise to make space.

6. Below that should be the message you want to communicate to the Manufacturer that will interest him or her in calling you with the inventories they have on hand. Whatever you say, the following - or some version of it - should be in the body of the communication somewhere "We (or our company) specialize(s) in buying unwanted, outdated or overstocked merchandise for CASH. We buy total inventories and can keep the products out of your normal market place."

7. Finally - make sure that your address is at the bottom of the card with your telephone number, fax number and any email or web site address that you may have. This is important as it makes it possible for manufacturers to contact you.

The above are the basic things that should be on a postcard before you send it out to the manufacturers.

Mailing list

When purchasing a mailing list you should call several mailing companies. Their prices vary quite a lot, so shop around and buy the cheapest list you can find. All you want on the labels are the name of the company and the address.

You can have the company put a line like "Attn: Operations Manager / Owner" as the top line on each label at no extra charge to you. It is normally cheaper to buy 5000 labels even if you use them over a period of several weeks. Same thing goes for the post cards - it is usually cheaper to buy them in lots of 5000. In addition, shopping around applies here as well. Printers vary in their prices. Shop around; find a cheap one that does a good job. Once you have the cards and the labels, buy the postage stamps you need. Make sure that you get the self-sticking stamps - they are easier to apply than the ones you have to wet.

You can then go ahead and send out about 500 post cards a week over a period of 10 weeks and that should be enough to have manufacturing companies contacting you and offering you their excess inventories. When you get calls from Manufacturers, just make sure they are talking about completed consumer products and then continue the same as you would from point number 11 of the "locating by telephone" information above.

The advantage of locating products by telephone and mail/email is that you get immediate inventories by telephone.

By mail/email, you build up a residual line whereby the manufacturers are contacting you up to several months after you have done a mailing.

The reason for this is that when they receive the card initially, they did not have inventories available.

HOWEVER, they do save these cards and call you when they do!

Finally: However you go about getting these post cards out, check with the Post Office for the latest rules and make sure you follow them to the letter - this way everyone will be happy and everything will go all right with the mailing.

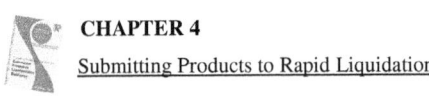

CHAPTER 4
Submitting Products to Rapid Liquidations

Once you have located an inventory, gotten agreement on the tentative price offer for the inventory and received the samples, this is your next step:

1. You can submit the information along with three samples to Rapid Liquidations so that we can attempt to sell them for you. If we are successful in selling the inventory, we will split the profits with you on a 50/50 basis. We will normally attempt to have the inventory sold and your 50% to you within 30 days of the completed and correct submission package arriving with us.

Or…

2. You can attempt to sell the inventory yourself. In which case you get to keep all the profit you can make.

To submit inventories to Rapid Liquidations for us to attempt to sell them for you, you need to do the following:

Make a submission form that has the following information on it:

• Your Name_____

• Your Phone Number _____ Your Address: _____

• The manufacturing company's Name_____ Phone Number_____

• Contact there_____

Product information:

• What is it? _____

• Where is it located? _____

• How is it packaged? _____

- What is the retail price? _____

- Wholesale price? _____

- Manufacturing cost? _____ .

- Price Manufacturer has agreed to sell for? _____

Send this completed submission form with three samples of the product, and a self-addressed stamped envelope so we can let you know of the results of our attempt to sell the inventory.

Send the whole package to

Clifford Woods

Rapid Liquidations

12000 Weddington Street, Suite #8

Valley Village, CA 91607

If you wish to sell the products yourself, then please go ahead and do so. To accomplish that you will need to locate buyers and offer them the inventory.

SUMMARY:

OK. The above is the basic information on locating completed consumer products at liquidation prices and submitting them to us to sell.

Currently, you are receiving this manual for way less than $100.00.

The reason for this is simple.

It is our hope that you will find this business interesting and want to do it. If that is that case and you decide to send us the inventories you find, then you will be helping us make money by selling the products and splitting the profit. We will be helping you get started in an interesting and rewarding business that has good potentials.

This is a win-win situation. Everyone wins!

BONUS:

There is a side bonus to this business and that is the samples. You will be receiving half a dozen samples of each inventory you work with. Three of these will be sent to us to pass on to buyers we are attempting to sell these products to. These samples will not be returned. However, you will still have three samples on hand.

You can use these for many different things:

1. Sending out to other buyers you may have collected to see if they are interested

2. Giving them away as presents to your relatives and friends

3. Selling them (note: please ensure you have the appropriate sales permit)

What you do with them is up to you. Whatever you choose to do with them, one thing is very certain: if you do as I have outlined in this manual, you will soon have more samples than you know what to do with!

Things like golf clubs, watches, and baseball caps, sponges, paperback books and hard cover books, shoes, clothes, leather jackets etc. will be arriving at your door in short order after starting this locating business.

Finally - If there is anything in this manual that is not clear or you want some more information about, please feel free to write or email us.

PO BOX 4176, VALLEY VILLAGE, CA 91617

EMAIL: CLIFF@RAPID-LIQUIDATIONS.COM

WE ARE ALWAYS HAPPY TO HEAR FROM YOU.

SAMPLE POSTCARD TEXT

WE BUY UNWANTED CONSUMER MERCHANDIZE FOR CASH!

Please copy and pass to: The Warehouse Manager, The Operations Manager, Inventory/Stock Manager and the Owner.

Dear Sir or Madam: As the person in charge of your area, you are responsible for the selection of the products your customers require. Customers being fickle and the changing times result in your being left with excess, outdated or discontinued merchandise. This is where we can be helpful.

Our Company, Rapid Liquidations, specializes in buying this merchandise for CASH. We purchase entire inventories and do have the ability to keep these out of your normal market place. When you have a moment and are not too busy, we would appreciate your having a look around to see if you have any merchandise sitting around that you would like to get rid of.

If you do find such merchandise, please call or write us. We can help you liquidate these excesses for cash now!

Sincerely,

(Your name) and (your company name) and email/website address

SAMPLE LETTER / FAX / EMAIL - TEXT

Date:

For the attention of:

Dear Sir or Madam:

As the person in charge of your area, you are responsible for the selection of the products your customers require. Customers being fickle and the changing times result in your being left with excess, outdated or discontinued merchandise. This is where we can be helpful.

Our Company, Rapid Liquidations, specializes in buying this merchandise for CASH. We purchase entire inventories and do have the ability to keep these out of your normal market place. When you have a moment and are not too busy, we would appreciate your having a look around to see if you have any merchandise sitting around that you would like to get rid of.

If you do find such merchandise, please call or write us. We can help you liquidate these excesses for cash now!

Sincerely,

(Your name)

(Your company name)

Email and website address ETC.

QUESTIONS AND ANSWERS

These are questions that have been asked and the answers to them. If you have other questions than these, please feel free to write to us at **Error! Hyperlink reference not valid.** above.

Question: I do not have the bucks to purchase the phone book so I have to wait until I do?

Answer: Check around in your local area to see if there are any sales organizations like telephone sales companies. These use these 800 directories and get the new ones as they come out. Some of them may have an older directory around that they may want to donate. Check it out. Also, check the internet - you should be able to find 800 number listings there free of charge.

Question: Do you have interest in other products outside of the ones listed in the Locator Manual?

Answer: Yes. The products listed in the manual are examples of the types of products we are interested in. We could not possibly list ALL Consumer Products - they are so many! Here is the basic guideline. If a product can be put on a shelf and sold retail, we are interested. This means that they have to be COMPLETE and RETAIL ready.

All a buyer would need to do with the products is put their price stickers on them and put them on the shelf for sale. So, ANY products that is complete and can be put on a shelf and sold retail is of interest.

If you find a product and are not sure what to do with it or if it fits the category of interest, just email us at MAILTO:INFO@RAPID-LIQUIDATIONS.COM, tell us about it and we will tell you if it is something we think can be sold by us. We will answer you quickly as well.

Question: If I wanted to buy and sell myself, what procedure would I use?

Answer: Very interesting question indeed. Basically, the key to buying and selling yourself is to have a list of people on your list that are interested in buying the products you are finding. This usually takes about three to six months to develop to a point where it would be viable. Developing such a list can be done several ways. One way is to send post cards to all the discount stores in the country and tell them what you have and find out if they are interested in being added to your list.

Another is to put the word out with your friends and family and tell them what you are doing and ask them to spread the word. Then there is newspaper advertising, editorials in the local newspapers and so on.

The main point here is that you can do this in various ways. The catch is that it takes from three to six months to get enough people on your list to make it worthwhile doing yourself.

Question: How are my commissions paid through your company?

Answer: Another important question. Basically, we get the details of a product you send in to us, create a product information sheet and send this out to the buyers we determine would be interested in a particular product.

Then when we get a buyer, we get them to send the money in to us for the inventory. We then send the funds to the owner of the inventory so that they can ship the inventory to the buyer.

Immediately after the funds have been sent to the Seller and we have confirmation that the goods have been shipped, we calculate the exact profit on the deal and divide it in two. You half is then sent to you. How it's sent to you is determined on an individual basis. Some folks like checks; others prefer bank wire transfers, etc.

Question: How do you see this industry in the future as far as growth potential and profit?

Answer: I see this industry as basically expanding at this time and in the future. It is a peculiar thing about this business that is generally does better the worst off the economy get.

The reason for this is that as the economy worsens more and more companies go out of business. When that happens, manufacturing companies get stuck with more products they have made that cannot be delivered.

This means more inventories for us to find and sell at a profit. In normal times, there is a certain percentage of goods that are overstocked and as things get worse economically, the "unwanted" factor of the business increases due to companies going bankrupt.

So, business and profits increase for us as well.

Question: Do I need to sign any fee or Commission agreement with your company?

Answer: The short answer to this is no. Our agreement is written in the manual. We split the profit right down the middle (50/50). That is all there is to it.

You can stop sending products to us to sell for you anytime you wish. There is no contract. As a matter of fact we expect a certain percentage of you to expand and start to sell the products you locate yourselves.

Others of you may not wish to get into the selling end of things and will just continue to locate products for us and we will continue to do our very best to sell them as quickly as possible.

Question: Is it illegal to send faxes to different manufacturers?

Answer: No - this is not illegal at the time of this writing, but check with your local laws to ensure you are following the laws of the land.

It is just that it would not be as effective as the methods outlined in the manual. The manual covers sending faxes in a certain way. You call, speak with the correct person and if they are not immediately available, get their name and fax number, get their permission to send them a fax and send them a fax.

You then save these names and fax addresses and build up a list of potential sellers, you can send other faxes to these names say, once every two months or so. Not more than that.

Remember that the majority of those receiving them save the faxes and you will hear from them eventually. Sometimes you do not hear from someone for 6 months!! But you eventually get a phone call or a letter.

These people save your information as they have NEED of your services. Just make sure you give them all the information as covered in the manual.

Question: How do you keep the merchandise out of the normal market place of the seller of the inventory?

Answer: To solve this, you do what is called 'restricted sales'. This basically means that you ask the manufacturer or inventory seller WHERE and in WHICH SHOP or CHAINS he does not want the merchandise to appear and then when you sell it, simply state that the inventory cannot be sold in the locations specified by the Manufacturer or inventory seller.

This makes an inventory harder to sell, but if there are not too many restrictions on it, you should be able to move it eventually.

Tip: The more restrictions on the inventory, the LESS you offer for it.

SPECIAL ADDITION:

Finding buyers and selling liquidation stock

Ok, so you have done everything in the locator's manual and you now have inventory samples coming in and you are sending these off to a company to sell and split the profit with.

Now you are ready for the next stage.

Finding the buyer and selling the products; keeping all the profit. All right, here are the facts of life with doing that. There are several stages involved. These are:

•Finding buyers

•Selling the products as a broker

•Graduating up to mainly being a liquidation broker.

FINDING THE BUYERS:

There are several ways to find buyers. One is to buy a mailing list of every discount and ninety nine cents store in the country and mailing each one a post card with the heading saying "Save 85% off retail Prices!!!" and briefly tell them that you are Liquidators and have consumer products (retail ready and factory fresh) and that you can sell these to them for 10 to 15% of retail price.

Then simply ask them if they would like to be added to your Fax or Email list so that you can notify them as inventories come in.

Make up a fax list and email list from the responses. Then as you get inventory information in, make up an information sheet and email and fax them out to the people on your list.

© 1998, 1999, 2000, 2001, 2013, 2015 and 2016 by Clifford Woods

Another way is to search the Internet search engines for "Liquidators" and contact them with a brief email simply saying that you are an independent locator and would like to know if they work with independent locators.

Also mention that you specialize is locating consumer products. You will get some responses from this and then add that to your list.

While searching, you will find some Liquidators that have free information listings where you can sign up and have FREE email notification from their members when they have products to sell. Sign up for these as they give you another source of building your email contacts.

SELLING THE PRODUCTS

Ok, so now you have your email and fax list being built up.

What you do now is start creating information sheets like this one - *New Product Information Sheet. (Next Page)*

> # NEW PRODUCT INFORMATION SHEET
> # PRODUCT NOW AVAILABLE FOR LIQUIDATION
>
> •Date: _____
>
> •Name: BACK SUPPORT BELTS
>
> •What is it? These are back support belts from Custom LeatherCraft ®. They are 100% factory-fresh, packaged in display box or clam shell pack. They are worn by anyone who lifts objects in their work or home.
>
> •Quantity: 6190 units (2922 Large, 1659 medium and 1609 small)
>
> •Retail Price: $29.95 ea. / Wholesale price $15.54 ea.
>
> •Liquidation Price: $3.25ea ($20,000.00 for entire inventory)
>
> Products are located in New Jersey
>
> Call of Fax for additional details and questions.
>
> Yours truly,
>
> (Your name)_____ (Your phone number/fax number and web site)"

Once you have a sheet created for a product you have decided to take on board, you simply fax these out to your fax list and email the same information out to your email list (add a picture of the product to the email list if you have a picture).

Make sure that the liquidation price you are quoting on your information sheet is MORE than you have agreed to pay the seller. The additional amount is YOUR PROFIT!

Guideline: when working out the liquidation price follow a simple rule - do not be greedy, it's better to sell lots of inventories with small profits than trying to sell a few inventories at HUGE profits.

Now, the responses start coming in with buyers wanting additional information or wanting samples etc. As you will have samples by now, you send the additional information and samples off as needed, but make sure the buyers are serious before sending out all your samples.

When a buyer wants to buy the inventory, this is the sequence:

1. Buyer sends you the money either by bank wire, check or credit card.

2. You bank it and make sure the finds are cleared and are actually in your hands.

3. You send payment to the seller in the form that he desires it with shipping instructions to ship the products to the buyer.

4. Make sure that the seller gets the funds and SHIPS the products and make sure the buyer gets it in good condition and is happy. This last step will ensure you have future happy buyers and sellers.

Note: The use of purchase orders is not mandatory but they do make things smoother. When a buyer wants an inventory, simply ask him to send a purchase order so you can hold the goods for him.

Once you have his purchase order, then you write one, from yourself, and send it to the seller so he holds the goods for you. After that is in place, you concentrate on getting funds in and out.

The above are the basics of the selling sequence.

GRADUATING UP TO A LIQUIDATION BROKER MAINLY

The next stage from there is something called a liquidation broker. This is where you offer your services to buyers and merchants and distributors who are looking for specific merchandise that they sell.

The deal is simply this - you find them whatever they want. They pay the cost of the item and shipping to their location plus pay you a broker's fee of 15% or 20% of the item bought — depending on if he is going to be an ongoing client of yours. Ongoing clients are usually charged 15% of the items bought.

One-off or a sporadic client is charged 20%. [You adjust these percentages to suit your market or the people you are dealing with.]

The way this is done is simply collecting names and addresses of buyers and distributors and offering your services as a liquidation broker that specialize in finding them "whatever they want or there is no charge."

Also, you will need to accumulate a list of Liquidators, manufacturers and brokers that you can email when a client has told you what he or she wants. There you go - that's the basics of this business.

Thank you for reading my manual. If you enjoyed it, won't you please take a moment to leave me a review at your favorite retailer?

Thanks!

Clifford Woods

You can contact me at the address above in the manual.

ABOUT THE AUTHOR

After high school, Clifford spent about 15 years studying the intricacies of organizations and businesses in the US and other countries and became a consultant. He consulted businesses and individuals to stellar results all over the world (USA, Canada, Sudan, South Africa, Belize), and mainly in Europe. He settled down in the United Kingdom.

He holds a bachelor's degree (equiv) in Business Administration. You can write to him any time.

As one individual he assisted recently stated" Clifford is the most logical and solution oriented person I have ever met. He analyzes every situation properly and design what is needed to resolve it and it works!"

In between Consulting, He has written and published Science Fiction Short Stories and a manual on the business of Liquidating Consumer Products. He continues to write in his spare time.

www.ingramcontent.com/pod-product-compliance
Lightning Source LLC
Chambersburg PA
CBHW070422190526

45169CB00003B/1367